ACCLAIM FOR JEFF SMITH'S

Named an all time top ten graphic novel by Time *magazine.*

"As sweeping as the 'Lord of the Rings' cycle, but much funnier." —*Andrew Arnold*, Time.com

★*"This is first-class kid lit: exciting, funny, scary, and resonant enough that it will stick with readers for a long time."* —Publishers Weekly, *starred review*

"One of the best kids' comics ever." —Vibe *magazine*

"BONE *is storytelling at its best, full of endearing, flawed characters whose adventures run the gamut from hilarious whimsy . . . to thrilling drama."*

—Entertainment Weekly

"[This] sprawling, mythic comic is spectacular."

—SPIN *magazine*

"Jeff Smith's cartoons are irresistible. Every gorgeous sweep of his brush speaks volumes."

—Frank Miller, creator of Sin City

"Jeff Smith can pace a joke better than almost anyone in comics." *—Neil Gaiman, author of* Coraline

"*I love* BONE! BONE *is great!*"

—Matt Groening, creator of The Simpsons

"Every one of the zillion characters has a unique set of personality traits and flaws and dreams that are developed amid the pandemonium."

—Kyle Baker, Plastic Man *cartoonist*

"BONE *moves from brash humor to gripping adventure in a single panel."* *—ALA* Booklist

"BONE *is a comic-book sensation. . . . [It] is a classic of writer-artist craftsmanship not to be missed."*

—Comics Buyer's Guide

Rock Jaw
Master of the Eastern Border

OTHER ***BONE*** BOOKS

Out from Boneville

The Great Cow Race

Eyes of the Storm

The Dragonslayer

Rock Jaw

Master of the Eastern Border

By Jeff Smith

with color by Steve Hamaker

An Imprint of

SCHOLASTIC

New York Toronto London Auckland Sydney Mexico City New Delhi Hong Kong

ISBN 978-93-5275-475-5

ACKNOWLEDGMENTS

Harvestar Family Crest designed by Charles Vess

Map of *The Valley* by Mark Crilley

Color by Steve Hamaker

First Scholastic edition, February 2007

This reprint edition: March 2026

Book design by David Saylor

Printed in India at VK Global Digital Private Limited

This book is for Krishna and Avaday Iyer

CONTENTS

- CHAPTER ONE -

ROQUE JA - - - - - - - - - - - - - - - - - - -1

- CHAPTER TWO -

THE ORPHANS - - - - - - - - - - - - - - - 23

- CHAPTER THREE -

RAT CREATURE TEMPLE - - - - - - - - - - - 45

- CHAPTER FOUR -

GHOST CIRCLES- - - - - - - - - - - - - - 67

- CHAPTER FIVE -

CALL OF THE WILD - - - - - - - - - - - - 93

BONE
LOOK!
THERE! DO YOU SEE IT? ISN'T IT BEAUTIFUL?
SNIFF IT'S A SANDWICH BEING BORN!
SSSS!
OKAY, YOU TWO! ENJOY YOURSELVES . . .

...BUT YOU BETTER MAKE THE MOST OF YOUR **SANDWICHES**, BECAUSE WE DON'T HAVE A LOT OF BREAD LEFT.
GOODY! GOODY! GOODY!

SERIOUSLY, SMILEY! WE CAN'T SPEND ANOTHER NIGHT OUT HERE, OUR FRIENDS'LL BE **WORRIED**. WE NEED TO START BACK TO TOWN **TODAY**!
BUT **FONE BONE**, WHAT ABOUT **BARTLEBY?**

BARTLEBY?! DON'T TELL ME YOU **NAMED** THAT LITTLE CUB?
SURE, I DID! WE HAVE TO CALL HIM **SOMETHING** - - DON'T WE, BARTLEBY?
SS!

HE'S A RAT CREATURE, SMILEY, AN' WE'RE TAKING HIM UP IN TH' MOUNTAINS TO TURN HIM LOOSE! NOW, DON'T FORGET THAT!!
HEY! NOT SO LOUD!

YOU WANT THE LITTLE FELLA TO THINK WE'RE ABANDONIN' HIM?

SMILEY!
OKAY, OKAY. I JUST THOUGHT HE NEEDED A NAME, THAT'S ALL.
MOBY DICK

BUT WHY BARTLEBY, FOR GOODNESS' SAKE?
HE LOOKS LIKE A BARTLEBY, SEE?
MOBY DICK

IF YOU SAY SO!
WILL YOU READ US SOME MOBY DICK? I WANNA TEACH TH' LITTLE GUY HOW TO TAKE A NAP AFTER LUNCH --
MOBY DICK

HEY! THIS IS A WORK OF ART, NOT A SLEEPING AID!
OOH! DEBATING ITS MERITS! EVEN BETTER!
OKAY, WE'RE READY!
MOBY DICK

FOR YOUR INFORMATION, MOBY DICK IS **NOT** A BORING BOOK!
FOR YOUR INFORMATION, THAT BOOK CAN PUT YOU IN A **COMA!**

THIS BOOK **STIMULATES** YOUR MIND! NOT **ONLY** IS THIS BOOK FULL OF **HIGH SEAS ADVENTURE**, BUT THE **REAL** JOY IN MOBY DICK IS THE PURE **ACT OF READING** ITSELF - -
Z

HO! HO! THAT'S PRETTY FUNNY, **I** SAY.
I ALWAYS LAUGH AT **THAT** ONE, YOU **BET.**
MOBY DICK

COMRADE! LOOK! ALL IS NOT LOST! IT IS HIM! THE SUCCULENT LITTLE BONE MAMMAL!

AND HIS COUSIN! AT LAST WE WILL HAVE ENOUGH FOOD TO GORGE OURSELVES!
LET'S SNEAK AROUND BEHIND THEM . . .

?

HISS!
WHAT?

WOW! RAT CREATURES!
SSS!
SURRENDER, SMALL MAMMALS!!

QUICK! READ 'EM SOME OF THIS!!
WHAT?
SS!

WHAT ARE YOU DOING?!
CALL ME ISHMAEL!
?

IT'S NOT WORKING! HERE! YOU TRY!
GO ON! READ IT!
UM.

"CALL ME ISHMAEL. SOME YEARS AGO - - NEVER MIND HOW LONG PRECISELY - - HAVING LITTLE OR NO MONEY IN MY PURSE, AND NOTHING PARTICULAR TO INTEREST ME ON SHORE . . ."

". . . I THOUGHT I WOULD SAIL ABOUT A LITTLE AND SEE THE WATERY PARTS OF THE WORLD - -"
THERE! I THINK THAT DID IT!

KA-LUNK
BONK

OH, FER CRYIN' OUT LOUD!
C'MON! LET'S GET OUTTA HERE!

MAYBE IT'S NOT MOBY DICK AT ALL -- MAYBE IT'S **YOU!**
OH, SHUT UP!

WAIT A MINUTE! WHERE'S BARTLEBY?!

BARTLEBY! C'MON! QUICK! LET'S GO!!

WHAT'S HE DOING? DOESN'T HE KNOW THOSE GUYS ARE **DANGEROUS?**
SMILEY . . .

THEY'RE HIS OWN **KIND**, REMEMBER? THAT'S WHY WE BROUGHT HIM UP HERE IN THE FIRST PLACE.

THIS WORKED OUT PERFECTLY.
WE SHOULD LEAVE.

ZZNK
SNORT!

OOOOW! WHAT HAPPENED?
THAT VOICE!

. . . IT JUST DRONED ON AND ON . . . AND ON!
IT WAS HORRIBLE!

SAY! WHERE'D THEY GO?! WHERE'D THE BONES GO?

THERE THEY ARE!

UH, OH!
HERE THEY COME!
JUMP!
WUMP!
ooh!

UP YA GO!

GIVE ME YOUR HAND!
C'MON!

OH, NO! IT'S A DEAD END!
OOPS.

GOTCHA!

POW!
YEAH!
GO, BARTLEBY!

CHUNK
GET OFF OF ME, YOU BRAT!
KNOCK THE LITTLE TRAITOR'S HEAD IN!
HEY!

HISS!
AAARR!
AAAAA!

CLUNK!

WA-HOO! WHAT HIT ME?!
GO! GO!
RUN!
GET 'EM!
GET OUTTA HERE, YOU RATS!
SSS!

GO ON!! GET LOST!!!
WE DON'T WANT YOU AROUND HERE!
OKAY! OKAY! THEY'RE GONE!

DID YOU SEE THAT, FONE BONE? HE SAVED US! YOU SAVED US, BARTLEBY! OH, BOY! EVERYTHING'S GONNA BE ACES FROM NOW ON!
HMM.

WHAT'S THE MATTER, CUZ? EVERYTHING'S GONNA BE ACES FROM NOW ON, RIGHT? HE SAVED US!
WELL . . .
PAT PAT

THE WHOLE REASON WE CAME UP HERE WAS TO GIVE BARTLEBY BACK TO THE RAT CREATURES, AND LOOK WHAT HAPPENED!
YEAH. THAT DIDN'T WORK OUT TOO GOOD, DID IT?

NOW I DON'T KNOW WHAT WE'RE DOIN'.
AT THE MOMENT, YOU ARE TRESPASSING.

WHOA!
WELL, WELL.
WHAT A VERY UNUSUAL GROUP YOU ARE.
WHAT HAVE WE HERE? A RAT CREATURE CUB?

YOU CAN PUT DOWN THOSE ROCKS . . .
IT WILL TAKE MORE THAN A FEW STONES TO CHASE ME AWAY.

SO . . . ?
. . . ARE YOU WITH THEM?

OR
HIM?

WE, UH...
WHO'S THEM?
WHO'S **HIM?**

COME, COME...
YOU KNOW...

... **THEM!** THE OLD COW WOMAN AND THE **DRAGONS.**

... OR **HIM.**
SURELY YOU KNOW OF **HIM** -- THE **MASTER** OF THE RAT CREATURES -- **THE HOODED ONE!**

GULP!
THE VALLEY IS DIVIDED IN **TWO...**
EVERYONE **MUST** CHOOSE A **SIDE!**

WHY?
WE'RE STRANGERS IN THE VALLEY-- ALL WE WANT TO DO IS **RETURN** THIS LOST CUB BACK TO HIS HOME IN THE MOUNTAINS, MISTER-- UH... MISTER--?

I AM ROQUE JA, MASTER OF THE EASTERN BORDER. EVERYTHING YOU SEE IN THESE MOUNTAINS BELONGS TO ME.
HISS!

ANYTHING THAT MOVES IN MY DOMAIN, DOES SO ONLY WITH MY LEAVE. . .
AND THAT INCLUDES RAT CREATURES!

OKAY, OKAY, MR. ROCK JAW! WE DON'T WANT TO MESS WITH YOUR DOMAIN- - WE JUST WANNA TAKE TH' KID HOME!
SO, YOU ARE STRANGERS IN OUR VALLEY. . .

YEAH, WE'RE- -
..UH..
HOW INTERESTING.

FONE BONE! WE DON'T LIKE THIS GUY. . .
BONE, DID YOU SAY?

THE HOODED ONE IS SEARCHING FOR SOMEONE NAMED BONE . . .
HE IS?
YES. THE ONE WHO BEARS THE STAR IS NAMED BONE.
DO YOU KNOW HIM, PERHAPS?

A **STAR?** HEY! I THINK HE MEANS **PHONEY BONE!** WHAT'S HE WANT WITH **HIM?**
YEAH! HOLD IT RIGHT THERE, ROCK JAW!
R-R-ROQUE JA! R-R-ROQUE! YOU'RE NOT ROLLING THE **R!**

WHAT'S THIS HOODED GUY WANT WITH OUR COUSIN?

THE VALLEY IS **DIVIDED**, YOU SEE, EVER SINCE THE FALL OF THE KINGDOM, AND THE HOODED ONE SEES IT AS RIPE FOR **PLUCKING.**
BUT HE FEARS THAT A NEW **LEADER** WILL ARISE AND **UNITE THE VALLEY** BEFORE HE CAN **CONQUER** IT.

HOWEVER, IF YOUR COUSIN LOOKS ANYTHING LIKE **YOU TWO**, I HARDLY THINK HE'LL BE A **THREAT!**

ARE YOU TELLIN' ME THAT THE HOODED ONE THINKS **PHONEY BONE** IS GONNA **UNITE THE VALLEY?**
HA!

PHONEY'S NO **LEADER!** HE GOT CHASED OUT OF **BONEVILLE** JUST FOR SAYIN' HE WANTED TO RUN FOR **MAYOR!**
THAT'S ENOUGH, SMILEY.
WHO'S SIDE ARE **YOU** ON, ROCK JAW?

I THINK YOU ARE HARDLY IN A POSITION TO ASK QUESTIONS . . .
IS THAT RIGHT?

C'MON, SMILEY. LET'S GET OUT OF HERE!
YEAH. WE'RE WITH YOU!
YOU - -

- - ARE COMING WITH ME!
RUN!

WHAP!
AAAAAH!

LOOK OUT!

ERK!

TWO BONES AND A RUNAWAY RAT CREATURE.

I IMAGINE THERE WILL BE A SIZABLE REWARD FOR BRINGING THE THREE OF YOU IN. . . .

BUT I DON'T WANT ANY MORE DIFFICULTIES, SO SEND THE CUB UP FIRST.

YOU'RE NOT GONNA SEPARATE US!
THE CUB. NOW.

FORGET IT! YOU'LL NEVER GET THIS CUB!
ERF....

GO ON AN' LEAVE US ALONE! WE DIDN'T DO ANYTHING TO YOU!

I AM WAITING.

SMILEY----
URK

WHA--
BARTLEBY! WHAT ARE YOU --?

SIGH.

I'M GLAD SOMEONE IS BEING REASONABLE.

COME ALONG.

ISN'T THAT MUCH BETTER?

BONE
NOW WHICH WAY?
UM . . .
ARE WE LOST AGAIN?
LOOK AROUND . . . THERE'S GOTTA BE SOMETHING - -
WHERE?
THERE!

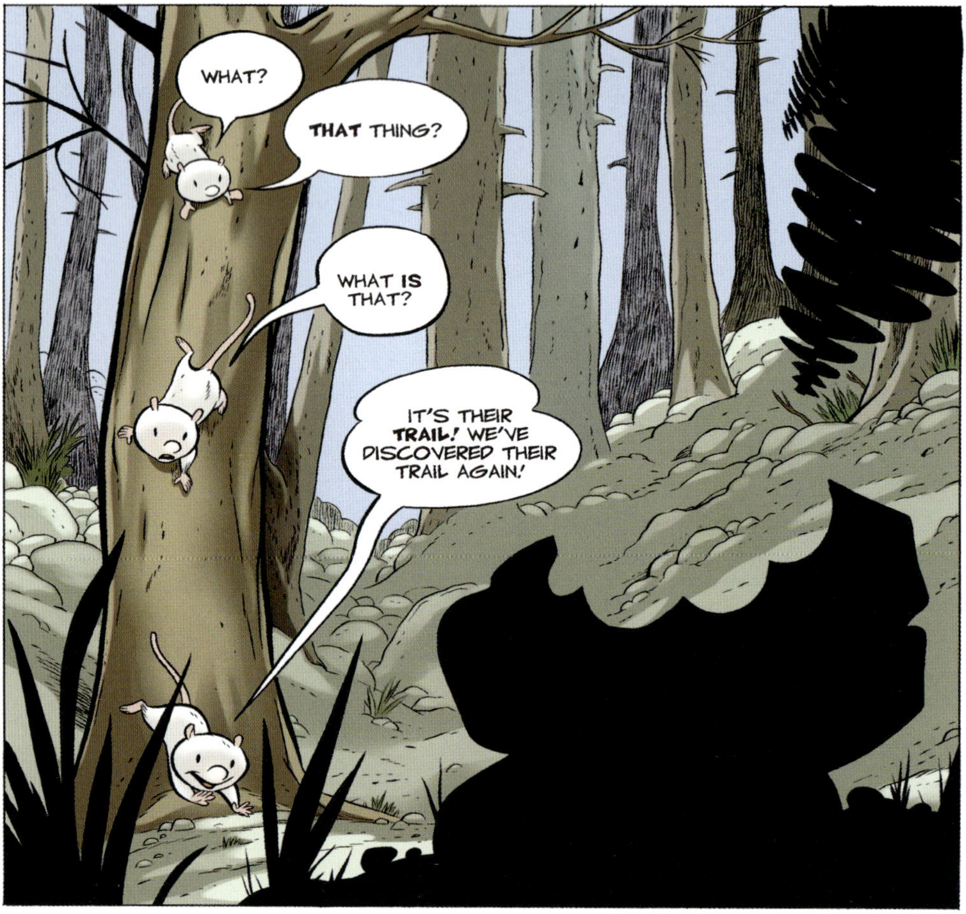

WHAT?

THAT THING?

WHAT **IS** THAT?

IT'S THEIR **TRAIL!** WE'VE DISCOVERED THEIR TRAIL AGAIN!

AND LOOK AT THAT!
EEYUH!
ONE OF SMILEY'S CIGAR STUBS!

I TOLD YOU WE WERE ON THE RIGHT TRAIL!
C'MON! THEY CAN'T BE FAR NOW!
I DUNNO . . .

WHAT?
AREN'T YOU COMIN'?
MM...

WE'RE PRETTY FAR FROM HOME. MOM'S GONNA BE MAD!
YOU'RE NOT SCARED, ARE YOU? JEEZ! WE'VE ALREADY COME THIS FAR!

BUT WHAT IF SHE'S WORRIED ABOUT US?
WHAT ABOUT FONE BONE AND SMILEY BONE? WHO'S GONNA WORRY ABOUT THEM? THEY DISAPPEARED DAYS AGO!

BUT MOM SAID NEVER TO GO NEAR TH' EASTERN MOUNTAINS 'CAUSE IT MIGHT BE DANGEROUS - -
SNAP!
WHOOPS.
WHAT'S THAT?

OHMYGOSH.
WHAT IF IT'S A--
SNK!
RUSTLE!
RUSTLE!

WHAT IF IT'S A 'POSSUM-EATING BEAR?
A 'POSSUM-EATING BEAR?!!

PLOP!

CRNCH!
CRUNCH!
RUSTLE!
RUSTLE!

SNIFF? SNIFF?

HEY!
WAKE UP, GUYS!
IT'S NOT A BEAR!
IT'S A RACCOON!

LISTEN, YOU! WHAT'S A RACCOON DOING SNEAKIN' AROUND IN THE MIDDLE OF THE DAY?
I DIDN'T MEAN TO SCARE YOU. ARE YOU OKAY?
WE'RE FINE! WE WERE JUST PLAYIN' POSSUM!

YOU DON'T NEED TO BE EMBARRASSED. MY NAME IS RODERICK.
WHY'D YOU SNEAK UP ON US LIKE THAT, RODERICK?

I WASN'T SNEAKIN' UP ON YOU!
THEN WHAT WERE YOU DOIN' IN TH' BUSHES? HIDIN' FROM YOUR MOMMY?
YEAH, WHAT WERE YOU DOIN'? HIDIN' FROM YER MOMMY?!

I DON'T HAVE A MOMMY OR A DAD, SO SHUT UP!
OOPS.
OH, MAN. ARE YOU AN ORPHAN?

WE'RE SORRY!
WHAT HAPPENED TO YOUR FOLKS?
THEY'RE DEAD! AN' FOR THE LAST TWO DAYS, I BEEN SPYING ON THE GUYS WHO DID IT!

?
?
COME WITH ME. I'LL SHOW YOU.

LOOK RIGHT THERE!

THE RAT CREATURES!

THE RAT CREATURES KILLED YOUR MOMMA AND POPPA?
YEP. THEY ATE MY MOM AND DAD.
THEY ATE 'EM?
MAN! THAT'S HARSH!

THOSE DORKS! YOU CAN'T GO AROUND EATIN' OTHER PEOPLE!
WELL, THEY ARE CARNIVORES!
JEEZ!
WE'RE TALKIN' ABOUT YOUR PARENTS, FER GOSH SAKES!

SNIFF.
I MISS MY MOMMA.
NOW LOOK WHAT YOU'VE DONE!
HEY, I DIDN'T EAT HIS FOLKS!
C'MON! I SAY WE TEACH THOSE RATS A LESSON!

BUT WHAT CAN WE DO? THEY'RE SO MUCH BIGGER THAN WE ARE!
WE CAN FIND FONE BONE AND SMILEY! THEY'LL HELP US!

WE WERE ON THEIR TRAIL ANYWAY! THEY CAN'T BE THAT FAR!
LET'S GO!

HOLD UP!
HOLD UP!

WHAT THE HECK?

IT'S THEM!
SLAP!
Shh!

WHERE ARE WE GOIN'?

YOU'LL FIND OUT SOON ENOUGH.

HE SAID HE WAS GONNA TURN US IN FOR A REWARD! I THINK OL' ROCK JAW, HERE, IS TAKIN' US TO THE RAT CREATURES!
I THINK SO, TOO.

YOU KNOW, ROCK JAW, FOR SOMEONE WHO CLAIMS TO BE MASTER OF THE EASTERN BORDER, YOU SURE SEEM TO BE KOWTOWING TO TH' RAT CREATURES AN AWFUL LOT.

MY NAME IS ROQUE JA, NOT ROCK JAW, AND YOU NEEDN'T WORRY ABOUT WHERE MY SYMPATHIES LIE . . .

. . . YOU SHOULD WORRY ABOUT YOUR OWN POSITION, MR. BONE.
IT WILL BE MUCH EASIER FOR YOU IN THE END IF YOU JUST CHOOSE A SIDE.
YEAH, YEAH.

PAT!
HEY!

WHAT WAS THAT FOR, ROCK JAW?
I THOUGHT I TOLD YOU NOT TO WALK ON THE SAME SIDE AS THE RAT CREATURE CUB.
IS THAT ALL YOU THINK ABOUT? SIDES?

THERE IS A WAR GOING ON. YOU WILL NEED TO CHOOSE A SIDE!
NOT EVERYONE WANTS TO CHOOSE SIDES, YA KNOW!
SO BACK OFF!
RIGHT! THERE MIGHT BE OTHER SIDES THAT WE WANT TO CONSIDER!

SUCH AS INSIDE VERSUS OUTSIDE?
WHOOP!
I'M MORE AN OUT-DOORSY TYPE, MYSELF!

HOW RUGGED OF YOU.

WHOA.
WHO'S THAT?
I DUNNO . . .

. . . BUT THEY GOT AWFUL BIG NOSES!
NOT THEM! WE KNOW WHO THEY ARE! THAT'S FONE BONE AND SMILEY BONE!
WHAT ARE YOU, A STUPE?

YEAH! WHO'S HIM?
WHO'S TH' BIG LION?
YEAH! WHAT ARE YOU, A STUPE?
YOU MEAN ROQUE JA? HAVEN'T YOU EVER SEEN ROQUE JA BEFORE?

NO. WE'RE FROM THE VALLEY! IS HE A GOOD GUY OR A BAD GUY?
WHAT DO YOU MEAN?
IS HE GONNA HELP OUR FRIENDS OR HURT 'EM?

I GUESS THAT DEPENDS ON WHOSE SIDE YOUR **FRIENDS** ARE ON.
WHOSE **SIDE?**

ROQUE JA SAYS EVERYBODY HAS TO BE ON A SIDE NOW BECAUSE IT'S A **WAR.** YOU CAN EITHER PICK THE **RAT CREATURES** OR THE **DRAGONS.**
I PICK THE **DRAGONS . . .**

. . . I'VE NEVER **SEEN** A **DRAGON**, BUT I KNOW I DON'T LIKE THOSE **RAT CREATURES!**
WELL, WE'RE NOT ON THE RAT CREATURES' SIDE **EITHER!**
BUT WHOSE SIDE IS **HE** ON?

ROQUE JA?
EVERYBODY KNOWS ROQUE JA **HATES** DRAGONS - -
UH, OH!

I THINK THE **BONE COUSINS** ARE IN **TROUBLE!**

HIT A NERVE, THERE ROCK JAW? WELL, IF YOU THINK WE'RE GOING TO DO ANYTHING THAT WILL HELP THE RAT CREATURES, YOU CAN FORGET IT!
THAT'S RIGHT! WE'RE FRIENDS OF THE VALLEY PEOPLE AN' WE'LL STOP YOU!

THE VALLEY PEOPLE . . . HA!

THE VALLEY PEOPLE MAY HAVE RULED IN THE PAST, BUT THEY LOST CONTROL A LONG TIME AGO.

THIS WAR IS NOW BETWEEN TWO OF THE ORIGINAL INHABITANTS OF THE VALLEY:
. . . THE HIGH AND MIGHTY DRAGONS . . .

. . . AND THOSE MISERABLE VERMIN THE RAT CREATURES!

CREEEK!

EH?

SHH! SHH!
BE CAREFUL! THE LOG IS SLIPPING!
WHAT DO I DO? WHAT DO I DO?

QUIETLY -- QUIETLY --
TAKE IT EASY.
JUST JUMP OVER TO THAT LITTLE BRANCH!

HMM.

I THOUGHT I HEARD SOMETHING . . .

. . . BUT IT MUST HAVE BEEN SOME FALLING ROCKS.

NOW WHAT WAS I SAYING? OH, YES . . . THE RAT CREATURES ARE VERMIN!
THEY ARE A POX!

THEY'RE A PESTILENCE! AND EVERY DAY MORE OF THEM ARRIVE FROM PAWA AND RUN AMOK IN MY BEAUTIFUL MOUNTAINS.
OH, BROTHER. THERE GOES THE NEIGHBORHOOD!

JUST THE SIGHT OF THEM ON MY MOUNTAIN INFURIATES ME!

C'MON!
I GOT AN IDEA!

YOU FIND ANYTHING OVER THERE, COMRADE?
NOTHING, COMRADE. THESE TINY BONES HAVE BEEN PICKED CLEAN!

BUT I'M SO HUNGRY, COMRADE! IT HAS BEEN DAYS SINCE WE ATE THOSE TWO RACCOONS!
I KNOW, COMRADE. I'M EVEN BEGINNING TO WISH WE HAD SOME OF YOUR HOMEMADE QUICHE!

OH, COMRADE! DO YOU MEAN IT?
HEY - - HEY! NONE OF THAT!
IF YOU EVER TELL ANYONE I SAID THAT, I'LL DENY IT!

HEY, RAT CREATURES!
YOU LOOK LIKE A COUPLE OF HUNGRY GENTLEMEN. . .

HOW ABOUT EATING US FOR DINNER?
!

IF YOU'RE NOT TOO FAT AN' LAZY TO CATCH US, THAT IS!
SSSS!
HOLD IT!

THEY'RE JUST TRYING TO GET A RISE OUT OF YOU, COMRADE! BESIDES, THEY ARE LITTLE AND MUCH TOO QUICK FOR US! WE WILL HAVE TO OUTWIT THEM!

WHAT'S TH' MATTER? I THOUGHT YOU WERE MEAT EATERS, NOT QUICHE-EATING OLD LADIES!
!

WHO ARE YOU CALLING QUICHE-EATING OLD LADIES?!
NOW? SHALL WE OUTWIT THEM NOW?

COME BACK HERE, YOU LITTLE BRAT! I'LL SHOW YOU WHO'S A QUICHE-EATING OLD LADY!!
WAHOO!
YES! COME BACK! WE'LL OUTWIT YOU TO DEATH!

IF YOU DON'T LIKE RAT CREATURES SO MUCH, WHY DON'T YOU TEAM UP WITH THE DRAGONS AND CHASE THEM OFF?
BECAUSE THE ONLY THING WORSE THAN THE RAT CREATURES ARE THOSE ARROGANT DRAGONS!

DO YOU KNOW WHAT THE VALLEY PEOPLE THINK ABOUT THE DRAGONS? THEY THINK THE DRAGONS CREATED THE VALLEY!!
SO?

SO, THEY THINK THE QUEEN OF THE DRAGONS WENT MAD ONE DAY, AND ALL THE OTHER DRAGONS WERE FORCED TO COME AND RESTRAIN HER . . .
SHE RESISTED, AND OUR LANDSCAPE IS THE RESULT OF THEIR BATTLE - - THEY CRASHED AND PUSHED AGAINST THE MOUNTAINS, AND CREATED THE VALLEY. IN THE END, WHEN THEY COULD NOT STOP HER, THEY HAD TO TURN HER TO STONE!

IF YOU ASK ME, IT'S A FOOLISH FAIRY TALE FIT ONLY FOR THE WEAK-MINDED.
DID YOU SAY SHE WAS TURNED TO STONE?
HEY!

HERE, KITTY KITTY KITTY!
!

HERE, KITTY KIT-- GRK!
AHA!

GOTCHA! NOW WHO'S A QUICHE EATING OLD--
UH, OH.

A RAT CREATURE! ON MY MOUNTAIN!
AAIIEEE!!

HELP!
EEK!
QUICK! OVER HERE!

C'MON!
SNAP!
IT'S SAFE BEHIND THIS ROCK!

ROAR!
I THOUGHT YOU SAID THIS WAS SAFE!
IT'S SAFE FOR US!

?
STOP MOVING, YOU IDIOT! DO YOU WANT THIS TREE TO COME LOOSE?!
CREEEK!

WUMP!
DON'T WORRY, COMRADE! I AM HERE TO SAVE YOU!

CREEEK!

STUPID, STUPID RAT CREATURES.
uh, oh...

AAAAAAAAAAAAAA
SMILEY! THE 'POSSUM KIDS ARE BACK THERE! ARE THEY OKAY?!

YES! THEY'RE SAFE!
WE JUMPED OFF THE LOG BEFORE IT SLID DOWN THE MOUNTAIN!
HA! HA! DID YOU SEE THAT LION'S FACE WHEN THE LOG FELL?

DID YOU SEE RODERICK WAVING HIS ARMS ON THAT ROCK? THAT TOOK GUTS!
I'M SO GLAD TO SEE YOU KIDS!
UH, OH! HEY, FONE BONE! I THINK ROCK JAW'S COMING BACK UP THE CLIFF!

COMING BACK UP?!! WOW! WE GOTTA GET OUTTA HERE!
RED ALERT! THAT CAT IS TEARIN' UP THE MOUNTAIN AN' HE'S CUSSIN' A BLUE STREAK!
RUN, RODERICK!
I CAN'T!

WE GOTTA GO NOW, KIDS!
WHAT DO YOU MEAN YOU CAN'T?
YOU HAVE TO COME WITH US! LET'S GO!
LET'S GO!
I CAN'T.

WHY NOT?
I CAN'T LEAVE THE OTHERS! BUT SINCE WE'RE ALL FRIENDS NOW, MAYBE WE CAN WORK TOGETHER!

FONE BONE!
WHAT'S GOING ON HERE, GUYS?!
WHAT OTHERS?
THEM! THE REST OF THE ORPHANS!

OH, BOY!
?!
THESE ARE MY FRIENDS!
COME OUT, EVERYBODY!

CHAPTER THREE RAT CREATURE TEMPLE

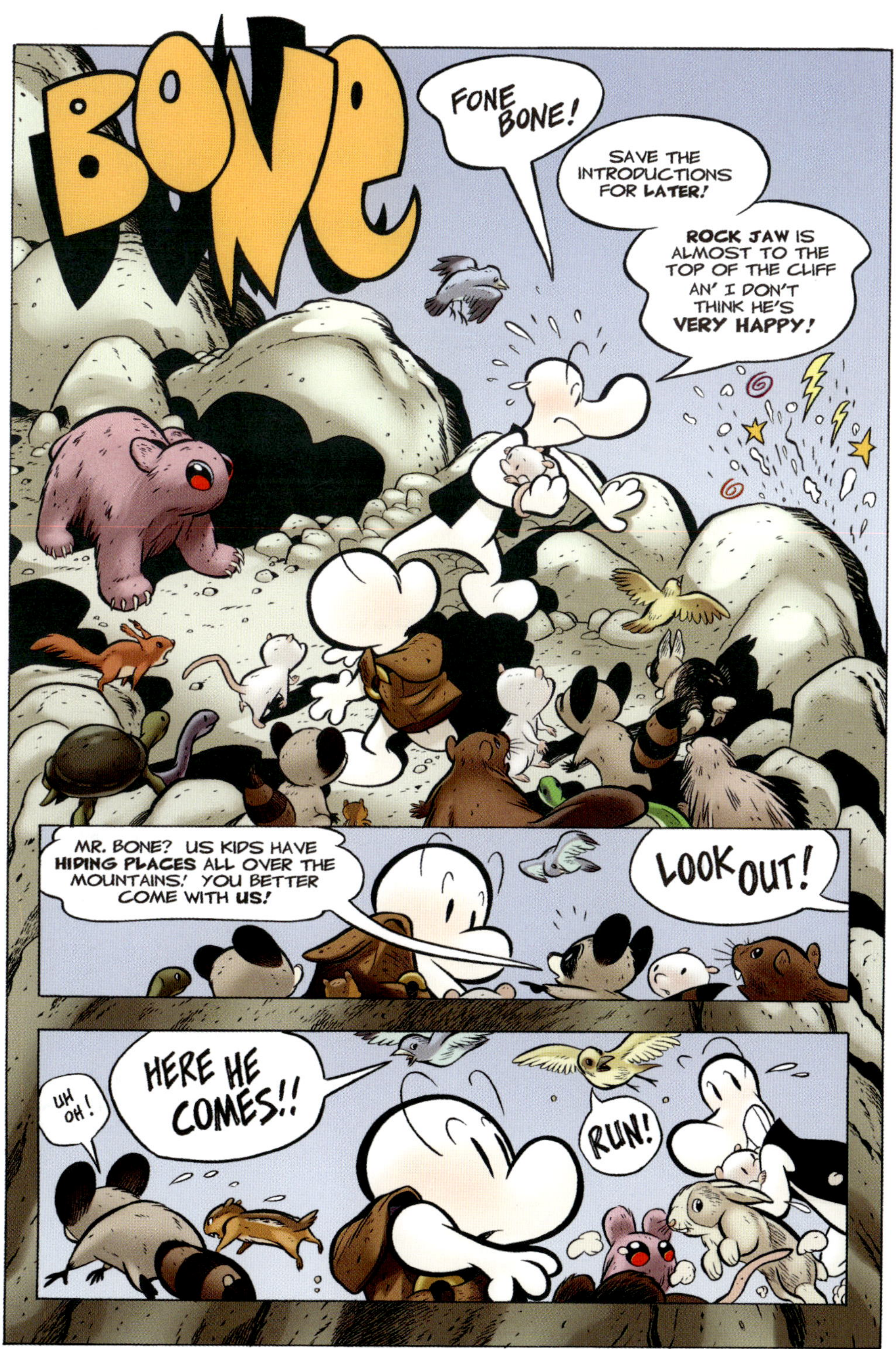

ROAR
C'MON, BARTLEBY!
GO! GO!

THIS WAY!
LOOK OUT! LOOK OUT!

HURRY!
YEEE!
SMASH!
CRASH

IN HERE, FONE BONE!

PANT PANT
WHEW!

HE CAN'T REACH US! WE'RE SAFE!

PEEK OUT AND SEE IF HE'S STILL THERE.
RIGHT!

HE'S STILL THERE.

WHAT ARE WE GONNA DO NOW?
WE MIGHT AS WELL GET COMFORTABLE . . . THAT GIANT CAT'S NOT GOING ANYWHERE! SCOOT OVER!
ROCK JAW WILL SIT THERE ALL DAY!

HE'LL SIT THERE FOR TWO OR THREE DAYS! HE'S DONE IT BEFORE!
OHMYGOSH! WE'RE TRAPPED!
IS THERE SOME OTHER WAY OUT OF HERE?

YES! THERE'S A TUNNEL!
IX-NAY! NOT IN FRONT OF TH' RAT!
YEAH! SHUT YER BEAK! YOU WANNA GIVE AWAY ALL OUR SECRETS?

SORRY!
NOW HOLD ON! THIS RAT CREATURE IS WITH US! AN' HIS NAME IS BARTLEBY!
HE'S JUST A BABY!
HE'S STILL A RAT CREATURE! AN' RAT CREATURES EAT PEOPLE LIKE US!
THEY ATE ALL OUR PARENTS!

WELL, WE CAME ALL THIS WAY TO RETURN BARTLEBY TO HIS HOME IN TH' MOUNTAINS, AN' WE'RE NOT GONNA ABANDON HIM NOW!
SMILEY. . .
IF TH' BONES SAY TH' KID IS OKAY, THEN HE'S OKAY!
OH, YEAH? AN' WHO ARE YOU?

THEY'RE MY FRIENDS! I TRUST 'EM!
HOLD IT! EVERYBODY JUST CALM DOWN! IT DOESN'T MATTER IF YOU TRUST US OR NOT. . .
WE CAN'T STAY TRAPPED IN THIS CAVE FOR TWO OR THREE DAYS!

TRUE! WE HAVE TO USE THE SECRET PASSAGE OR WE'LL STARVE TO DEATH IN HERE!
NOT IF HE EATS US FIRST!
THAT'S ENOUGH! SHOW US THE SECRET PASSAGE!

HERE IT IS!
IT LOOKS KINDA SMALL.
BE CAREFUL. IT GOES STRAIGHT DOWN.

LOOK OUT BELOW!
I'M GOIN' AFTER HIM! I DON'T WANT THOSE BIG TEETH BEHIND ME!
FINE! GET IN LINE!

SKRITCH!

SKRITCH!

WATCH IT. WE'RE IN SOME HUGE OPEN SPACE NOW.
SKRITCH

JUST A LITTLE FARTHER! WE'RE ALMOST THERE!

I HOPE SO. IT'S GETTIN' A LITTLE STUFFY IN HERE.
THIS IS IT, SMILEY! THIS IS THE OPENING! I'M OUTSIDE!
WHOA.

NOW THERE'S SOMETHIN' YOU DON'T SEE EVERY DAY!
YEAH, BOY.
HEY, SMILEY...

...YOU REMEMBER WHEN WE WERE WITH ROCK JAW, HE TOLD US A STORY ABOUT HOW THE VALLEY WAS CREATED?
YEAH, I REMEMBER. A BUNCH OF DRAGONS HAD A FIGHT AN' PUSHED UP THE MOUNTAINS.

RIGHT! THE QUEEN OF THE DRAGONS WENT MAD AND STARTED ON A RAMPAGE! THE REST OF THE DRAGONS WERE TRYING TO STOP HER!

AND TH' ONLY WAY THEY COULD DO IT WAS TO TURN HER TO STONE!
YOU MEAN...

THIS IS THE QUEEN OF THE DRAGONS TURNED TO STONE?!
NO, NO, NO! THIS ISN'T TH' QUEEN! THIS IS JUST AN ANCIENT TEMPLE OF SOME KIND --

UM.
AT LEAST I THINK IT'S JUST AN ANCIENT TEMPLE...

LISTEN, SMILEY! BEING TURNED TO STONE IS THE SAME THING THAT HAPPENED TO ANOTHER ANCIENT ENEMY OF THE DRAGONS! THE SAME ENEMY WHO IS AFTER PHONEY BONE AND THORN!

BUT I THOUGHT IT WAS A FAIRY TALE AN' NOBODY BELIEVED IN DRAGONS ANYMORE!
WE KNOW SOME PEOPLE WHO BELIEVE IN THEM - - LIKE GRAN'MA BEN AND LUCIUS DOWN! I'VE SEEN A DRAGON, TOO, REMEMBER?
THE LORD OF THE LOCUSTS IS AFTER PHONEY BONE AND THORN, AND HE WAS AN ANCIENT ENEMY OF THE DRAGONS WHO WAS TURNED TO STONE!

YOU MEAN TH' QUEEN OF THE DRAGONS AND THE LORD OF THE LOCUSTS ARE ONE AND THE SAME?
COULD BE. I DON'T KNOW. IT'S A WEIRD COINCIDENCE, ANYWAY.

SO . . . ? IS THIS JUST A TEMPLE OR NOT?
PRETTY SURE IT'S JUST A TEMPLE! MAYBE IT'S AN OLD RAT CREATURE TEMPLE. . .
IN ANY CASE, IT LOOKS ABANDONED NOW.

YEAH, YOU'RE RIGHT! IT'S JUST SOME OLD ABANDONED BUILDING! BESIDES, EVEN IF IT WAS AN OL' ENEMY OF TH' DRAGONS, HOW CAN IT HURT YOU IF IT'S TURNED TO STONE?
SAY, WHERE'D THE KIDS GO?
HEY, FONE BONE AND SMILEY BONE! OVER HERE!

WE'RE NOT OUT OF DANGER YET! RODERICK SAYS WE WON'T BE SAFE UNTIL WE REACH THE TREE LINE!
ONCE WE'RE IN TH' FOREST NO ONE CAN FIND US!

WHAT'S ROCK JAW UP TO?
HE'S STILL WATCHING THE UPPER ENTRANCE!
BUT HE'S STARTING TO GET SUSPICIOUS!
WE BETTER GET GOING.

IT'S A PRETTY STEEP CLIFF, BUT IT'S THE ONLY WAY DOWN FROM HERE, SO YOU BIG GUYS WILL JUST HAVE TO BE CAREFUL!

DON'T WORRY ABOUT US! WE CAN HANDLE IT!
LET'S GO!

THIS ISN'T SO STEEP!
WE'RE NOT TO THE STEEP PART, YET!

HEY, FONE BONE, HOW YOU COMIN' WITH YER LOVE POEMS?
MM?
HEY! HEY! I DON'T WANNA TALK ABOUT THAT IN FRONT OF EVERYBODY!

YOU WRITE LOVE POEMS, MR. BONE?
C'MON, BONE! TELL US A LOVE POEM!
uh...
YES! A LOVE POEM THAT YOU WROTE FOR MISS THORN!
WHAT MAKES YOU THINK MY LOVE POEMS ARE FOR THORN?

AW, HECK, BONE! EVERYONE KNOWS THEY'RE FOR THORN! JEEZ!
I'D LIKE TO HEAR A LOVE POEM, MR. BONE!
ME, TOO!
SURE! WE ALL WOULD!
FORGET IT! YOU'LL LAUGH!

COME ON! WE WON'T LAUGH! MAYBE WE CAN HELP WRITE ONE!
YES! WE WON'T LAUGH!
WE PROMISE!
WE'LL HELP WRITE YOUR LOVE POEM!
ALL RIGHT, ALL RIGHT. LET'S SEE . . .

OKAY, HERE'S ONE THAT ISN'T QUITE FINISHED YET.
AHEM.
IN THE STALLS OF MY HEART, DEAR, I'VE BUILT A HORSE-CART, DEAR, AND MY DEAR YOU CAN RIDE IT ALL DAY . . .

I'VE BUILT IT FROM LOVE - - - - FROM THE CLOUDS UP ABOVE - - E'EN THE RAINS CANNOT WASH IT AWAY!
BUT MY LOVE YOU CAN'T HEAR, SO THE CART WILL NOT STEER, AND I'M LEFT WITH A HEART FULL OF HAY.

WOW.
WAIT. I'M NOT DONE - -
HA! HA! HA! HA! HA! HA! HA!
LOOK AT BARTLEBY! HE'S COVERING HIS EARS!

EVERYBODY'S A CRITIC, HUH, CUZ?
HEY! HE CAN'T EVEN TALK!
HA! HA! HA! HA! HA! HA! HAW! HA!

YOU SAID YOU WOULDN'T LAUGH.
I'M TRYIN' NOT TO CRY!
YEA, BARTLEBY!
HA! HA! HA! HA
TH' RAT ISN'T SO BAD AFTER ALL!
HOORAY FOR BARTLEBY!
HA! HA!
HMMF!

HEY, NOW! WHAT'S THIS?
THIS IS THE STEEP PART.

YOU'RE KIDDING! WE CAN'T GO DOWN THIS, CAN WE?
LOOK OUT THERE.
YOU SEE THAT SMOKE?

OH, YEAH. WHAT DO YOU THINK THAT IS? A FOREST FIRE?
I DON'T KNOW.

WHERE ARE WE? IS THAT ANYWHERE NEAR THE VILLAGE?
I CAN'T TELL. WE'RE LOST, TOO. I THINK MAYBE THE VILLAGE IS UP THAT WAY.

YOU'RE FROM TH' MOUNTAINS, RODERICK! WHERE'S TH' VILLAGE OF BARRELHAVEN FROM HERE?
I'VE NEVER HEARD OF BARRELHAVEN BEFORE. SORRY.

WHAT DO YOU THINK, FONE? I MEAN WE DID LEAVE PHONEY BONE IN THE VILLAGE. YOU DON'T THINK ANYTHING COULD HAVE HAPPENED WHILE WE'VE BEEN AWAY?
HMM.

I THINK WE BETTER GET DOWN THERE.
SHOW US WHERE TO GO, KIDS.

WELL, WELL . . . IF IT ISN'T THE BONE COUSINS!

. . . AND THE LITTLE SNOTS WHO PUSHED US OFF THE CLIFF!
OH, NO! NOT AGAIN!

HEH, HEH, EXCEPT THIS TIME, THERE IS NO GIANT MOUNTAIN LION AROUND TO INTERFERE!
YESSS! ROQUE JA IS STILL KEEPING WATCH ON YOUR LITTLE MOUSEY HOLE UP ABOVE!

ANY LAST WORDS?

HEY!
SHOOo!

AAAH!
WHERE'D ALL THESE INSECTS COME FROM?
?
?

EEYUH!
GET 'EM OFF!

YOW!
LOOK OUT!

SO THERE YOU ARE!
EEEK! KINGDOK! YOUR MAJESTY!
YOU'RE ALIVE!

RRR.
Y-Y-YOU'RE LOOKING MUCH BETTER, YOUR HIGHNESS!
YESSS! YOUR ARM HOLE HAS HEALED QUITE NICELY!

YOU ARE DESERTERS!

DIE, TRAITORS!
AIEEE!
EEEE!

THUD!
FWAP!

SNAP!
WHERE IS EVERYBODY? IS EVERYBODY ON THE LEDGE?
CRACK
HELP!

THERE'S STILL TWO KIDS OVER THERE!

HELP!
BARTLEBY! WHAT ARE YOU DOING?!

HELP! HELP!

HE'S GOT 'EM!
C'MON! C'MON!

GNASH!

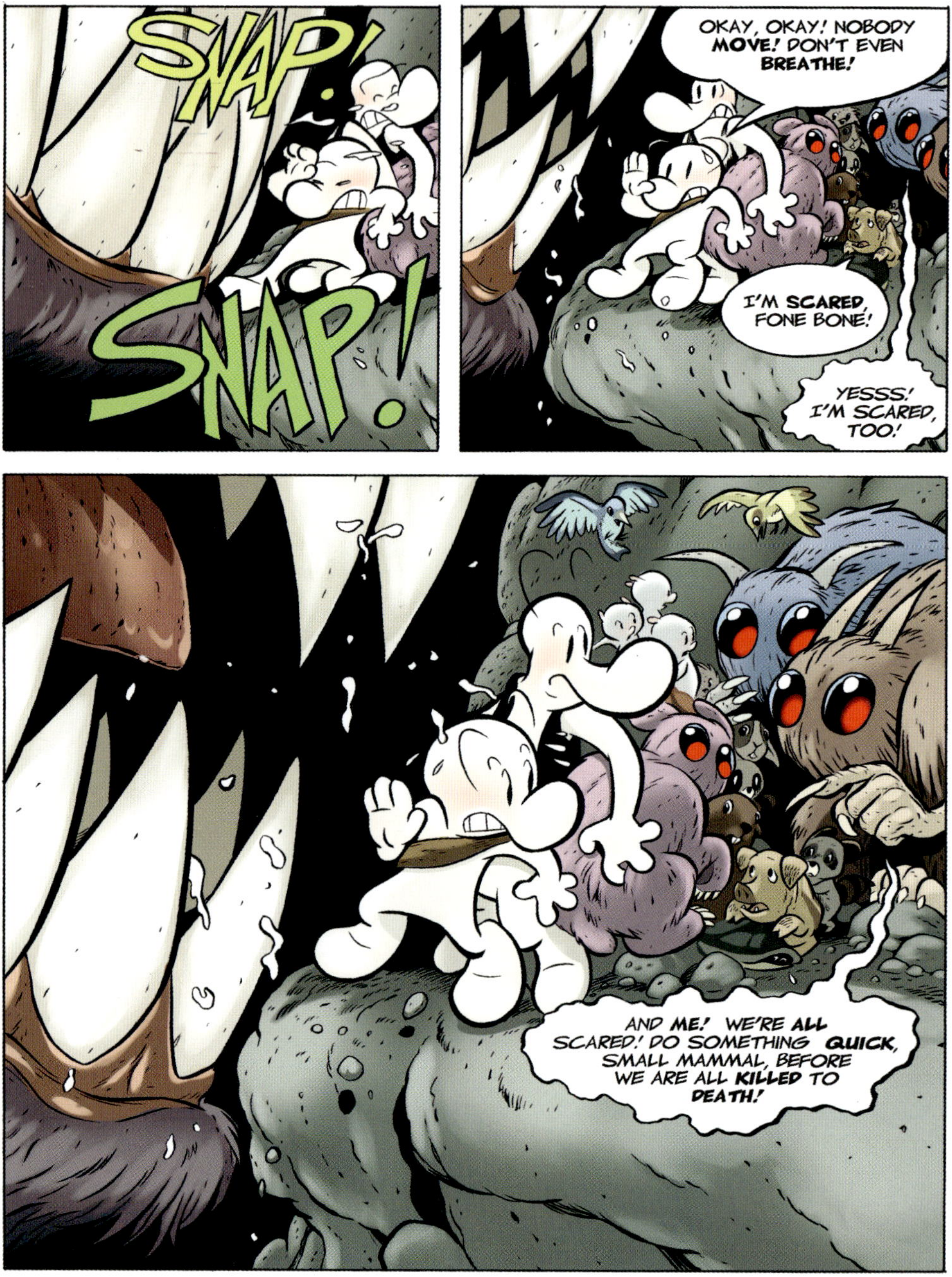

AND ME! WE'RE ALL SCARED! DO SOMETHING QUICK, SMALL MAMMAL, BEFORE WE ARE ALL KILLED TO DEATH!

BONE
RRRRR.
PUSH BACK, SMILEY!
I'M PUSHIN'! I'M PUSHIN'!
WE'RE TRAPPED BETWEEN A ROCK AND A SHARP PLACE!
THINK OF SOMETHING, SMALL MAMMAL! KINGDOK IS GETTING CLOSER WITH EVERY BITE!
YESSS! HURRY! I DON'T WANT TO DIE!
YOU THINK OF SOMETHING! HE'S YOUR KING, ISN'T HE?!!
WELL, NOT TECHNICALLY.
WE'RE DESERTERS.
SIR? MY FOOT'S ASLEEP!
DON'T MOVE IT!
THE SLIGHTEST MOVEMENT COULD PUT US INTO THE REACH OF THOSE TEETH!

THAT WAY! GO THAT WAY!!

THERE'S NOTHIN' THAT WAY EXCEPT FOR SHEER CLIFF FACE!

SO?!
WHAT DO YOU SUGGEST? DIPLOMATIC NEGOTIATIONS?!
WHY NOT? THE RAT CREATURES ARE DESERTERS! LET'S HAND 'EM OVER!

YEAH! KINGDOK SAID THEY WERE TRAITORS! MAYBE IF HE HAD THEM, HE'D LET US GO!
YEAH!
WAIT, NOW! LET'S TALK THIS OVER!

THROW 'EM TH' RATS!
GRRR!
RRR!
HELP US, SMALL MAMMAL!

SILENCE!

I AM NOT INTERESTED IN BARGAINING FOR THEIR MEANINGLESS LIVES!
YOU ALL WILL
DIE---

UNLESS . . .
UNLESS WHAT?

. . . UNLESS YOU TELL ME THE WHEREABOUTS OF THE ONE WHO BEARS THE STAR!
THE CHOICE IS YOURS . . .

DECIDE QUICKLY! MY PATIENCE IS RUNNING OUT!
THE ONE WHO BEARS THE STAR? THAT'S THE SAME NAME ROCK JAW USED FOR PHONEY BONE! WHY IS EVERYBODY AFTER OUR COUSIN?!
THEY THINK PHONEY WANTS TO BE LEADER OF THE VALLEY, REMEMBER?

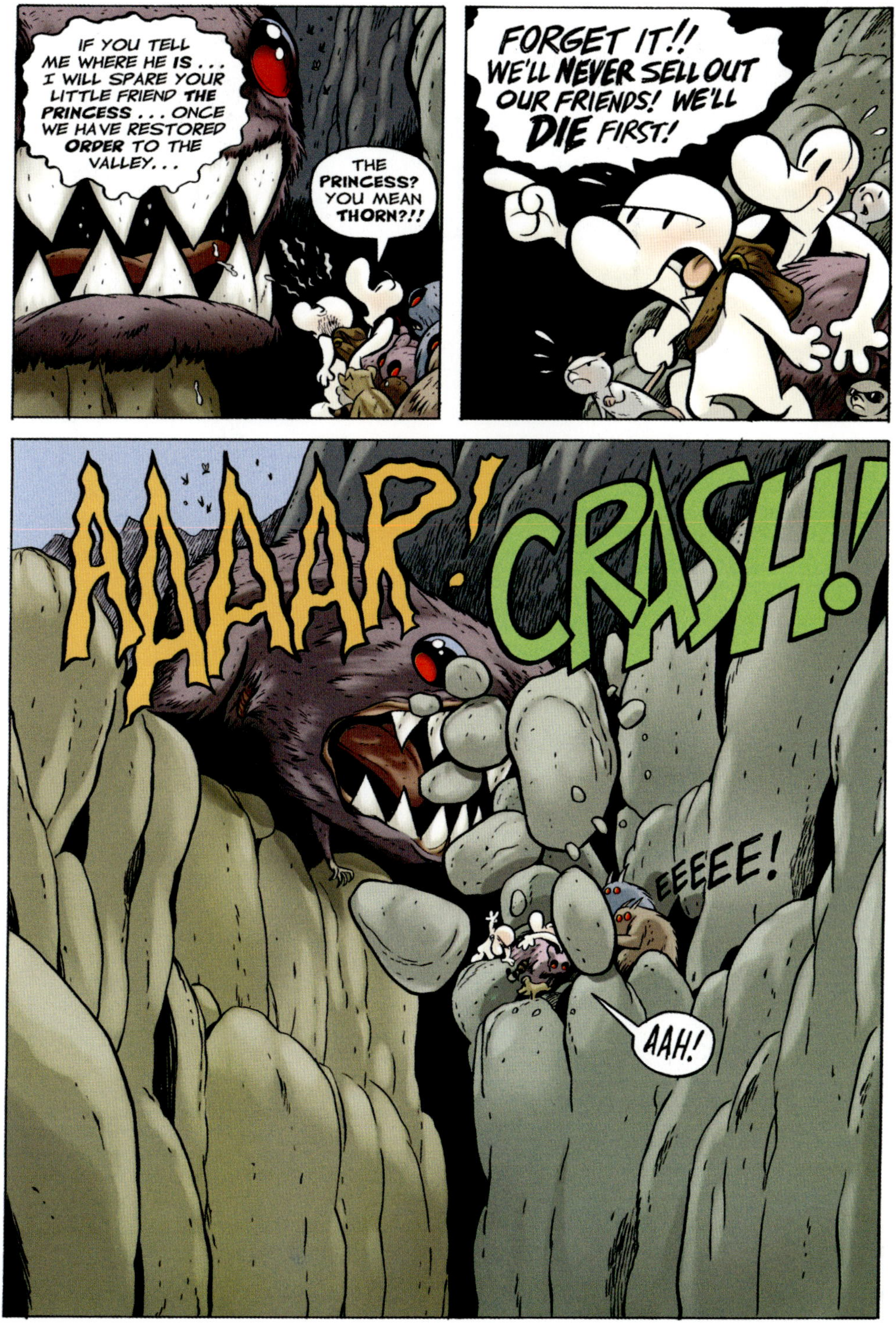

AAAAR! CRASH!

EEEEE!

AAH!

LOOK OUT! GO THAT WAY!

GRAB THAT KID!

COME ON!

I'LL GET YOU! YOU WON'T ESCAPE!
GIVE ME YOUR HAND!

KEEP GOING . . . FARTHER UP!

ALL RIGHT, THIS IS GOOD! HOLD UP!

EVERYBODY ACCOUNTED FOR?
WHERE'S RODERICK?

RODERICK'S MISSING? ANYBODY SEEN RODERICK?
I HAVEN'T SEEN HIM. HAVE YOU SEEN HIM?
MMM MMM!

HEY!
MM?

SMACK!
PTU!
RODERICK!

WHAT'S THE BIG IDEA EATING OUR FRIEND?
HISSS!
!

SMACK!

HEY! WHAT DID YOU HIT ME FOR?
WE'RE IN THE MIDDLE OF ESCAPING! CONTROL YOURSELF!

CONTROL MYSELF?!! I'M A MONSTER! MONSTERS DON'T CONTROL THEMSELVES! THAT'S THE WHOLE IDEA!!

WELL, YOU'D BETTER START, OR ELSE THESE NICE, LITTLE CREATURES WON'T HELP US ESCAPE FROM KINGDOK . . .

. . . WHO, BY THE WAY, SEEMS A LITTLE UPSET OVER THAT WHOLE ARM-CUTTING-OFF THING!
I NOTICED! HE SURE CAN HOLD A GRUDGE, CAN'T HE?
WE'RE NOT HELPING YOU ESCAPE!

REALLY?
WHY NOT?
BECAUSE YOU ATE ALL OUR PARENTS! THAT'S WHY NOT!

SEE? THAT'S WHAT I WAS SAYING! WE'RE NATURAL ENEMIES! TO US, YOU GUYS ALL LOOK LIKE HORS D'OEUVRES!
COULD WE DISCUSS THIS FROM A SAFER VANTAGE POINT? LIKE, SAY, A SLIGHTLY LARGER LEDGE?

I DON'T CARE WHAT ANYBODY LOOKS LIKE TO YOU FUZZ-FACE, JUST DON'T STICK 'EM IN YOUR MOUTH, GOT THAT?
YOU'RE NOT TH' BOSS OF ME!
HEY!

IT'S NOT GONNA TAKE KINGDOK LONG TO FIND US, SO HERE'S THE DEAL . . .
UNTIL WE'RE OFF THIS LEDGE, WE CALL A TRUCE! THAT MEANS WE ALL WORK TOGETHER!

IT ALSO MEANS NOBODY EATS ANYBODY! NO MATTER WHAT THEY LOOK LIKE!

HE'S TALKIN' TO YOU!
WATCH IT, BREAD-STICK!
WE AGREE TO YOUR TERMS, SMALL MAMMAL! NOW GET US OUT OF HERE!

KEEP AN EYE ON THOSE TWO, BARTLEBY!
CAREFUL!
I THINK WE CAN GO THIS WAY...

TOK
TOK!

HOLD IT!

OH, NO, OH, NO! NOW WHAT IS IT?
I THINK KINGDOK IS RIGHT ABOVE US!

WE'RE DOOMED!
HE'S JUST WAITING FOR US!

ALL RIGHT, ALL RIGHT! WE'RE NOT DOOMED YET! LET'S JUST THINK THIS THROUGH!

SOMEHOW WE HAVE TO GET TO THE SAFETY OF THE TREES DOWN THERE . . . BUT WE CAN'T GO STRAIGHT DOWN - - IT'S TOO STEEP!
AND WE CAN'T GO BACK, BECAUSE KINGDOK DESTROYED THE LEDGE!

UP IS OUT, BECAUSE THAT'S WHERE KINGDOK IS NOW!
YOU CALL THIS THINKING IT THROUGH?

WHATEVER YOU CALL IT, IT LEAVES ONLY ONE WAY OUT! FORWARD!
BUT- - BUT WE DON'T KNOW WHERE TH' LEDGE GOES!

YES! WHAT IF IT TAKES US RIGHT TO KINGDOK?
OR BACK TO ROCK JAW, THE GIANT MOUNTAIN LION! DON'T FORGET ABOUT HIM!
WHAT CHOICE DO WE HAVE?

HOLD ON- -
HEY, BIRD KIDS! CAN YOU SEE WHERE THIS LEDGE GOES?
THE LEDGE GETS SMALLER AND SMALLER!
BUT FARTHER AHEAD IS A BOULDER FLOW! IF YOU CAN REACH IT, YOU MIGHT BE ABLE TO WORK YOUR WAY DOWN TO THE TREES!

THIS IS INSANE!
IT'S STUPID!
HEY! NOTHING WE'VE DONE SO FAR HAS BEEN UN-STUPID, AND WE'RE STILL ALIVE, AREN'T WE?!

I CAN'T REALLY ARGUE WITH THAT, BUT I FEEL LIKE I SHOULD.
CARRY ON, FONE BONE! MAKE A STUPID DECISION!
RIGHT! FOLLOW ME!

LOOK OUT!
UH, OH. YOU HEAR THAT?
WE'VE HEARD THAT SOUND BEFORE!
ZZZZZ

IT'S KINGDOK'S LOCUSTS!
THEY'RE BACK!
EEE!
RUN!
THIS IS ALL YOUR FAULT!
MINE?! YOU'RE THE ONE WHO MADE US DESERT OUR POSTS! AND NOW WE'RE GOING TO BE PUNISHED!

THERE'S NO ESCAPE!
OH, WHY DID WE DESERT OUR POSTS?
AAAH!
YEE!

IGNORE THEM! THEY'RE JUST GRASSHOPPERS! THEY CAN'T HURT YOU!
WE HAVE TO KEEP MOVING!

HOLD ON TO THE CLIFF! DON'T PANIC!
AND WHATEVER YOU DO - -
AAH!

- - DON'T OPEN YOUR MOUTH!!
AAAH!
GAK!
PTT!
POO!

PTT PTT POO!
AAH!
AAH!
AAH!
GAK! POO
PTT POO!
PTT!
PTT!
GAK!

THERE'S TOO MANY! I CAN'T SEE!
BE CAREFUL! THEY'RE SWARMING ALL OVER THE LEDGE!
IT'S GETTING SLIPPERY!
SQUISH!

OH, GROSS
WHOOOP!
CRUNCH!
CRUNCH!

AAAAAAA

WHAT HAPPENED?
FONE BONE?!
OH, NO...

I THINK HE FELL OFF THE CLIFF!
FONE BONE?

HEY! THE LOCUSTS ARE LEAVING! I CAN SEE!
LOOK DOWN THERE!

IT'S BONE! AN' HE'S HURT!
OHMYGOSH.

OH, NO! THE LOCUSTS ARE ATTACKING HIM!
MOBY DICK

HEY!
MOBY DICK

WELL, WHAT DO YOU KNOW! THEY WEREN'T AFTER US AT ALL!
THEY WANT THAT BONE CREATURE! WHAT A RELIEF!
HANG ON, LITTLE PAL!

HELP ME, YOU GUYS!
BARTLEBY! GIVE ME YOUR PAW!
HURRY! I THINK THOSE BUGS ARE TRYING TO PICK HIM UP!

LOOK OUT!
ROAAAR!
!

IT'S KINGDOK! HE FOUND US!
GET BACK UP HERE!
AAAR
NO! I HAVE TO GET THOSE BUGS OFF MY COUSIN!

EEEK!
WOOF!
SNAP!

BARTLEBY! LET ME GO!!
THEY GOT HIM!

THEY'RE PICKING HIM UP!
OH, NO! WAKE UP, MAN!
HEY!

ZZZ

POW

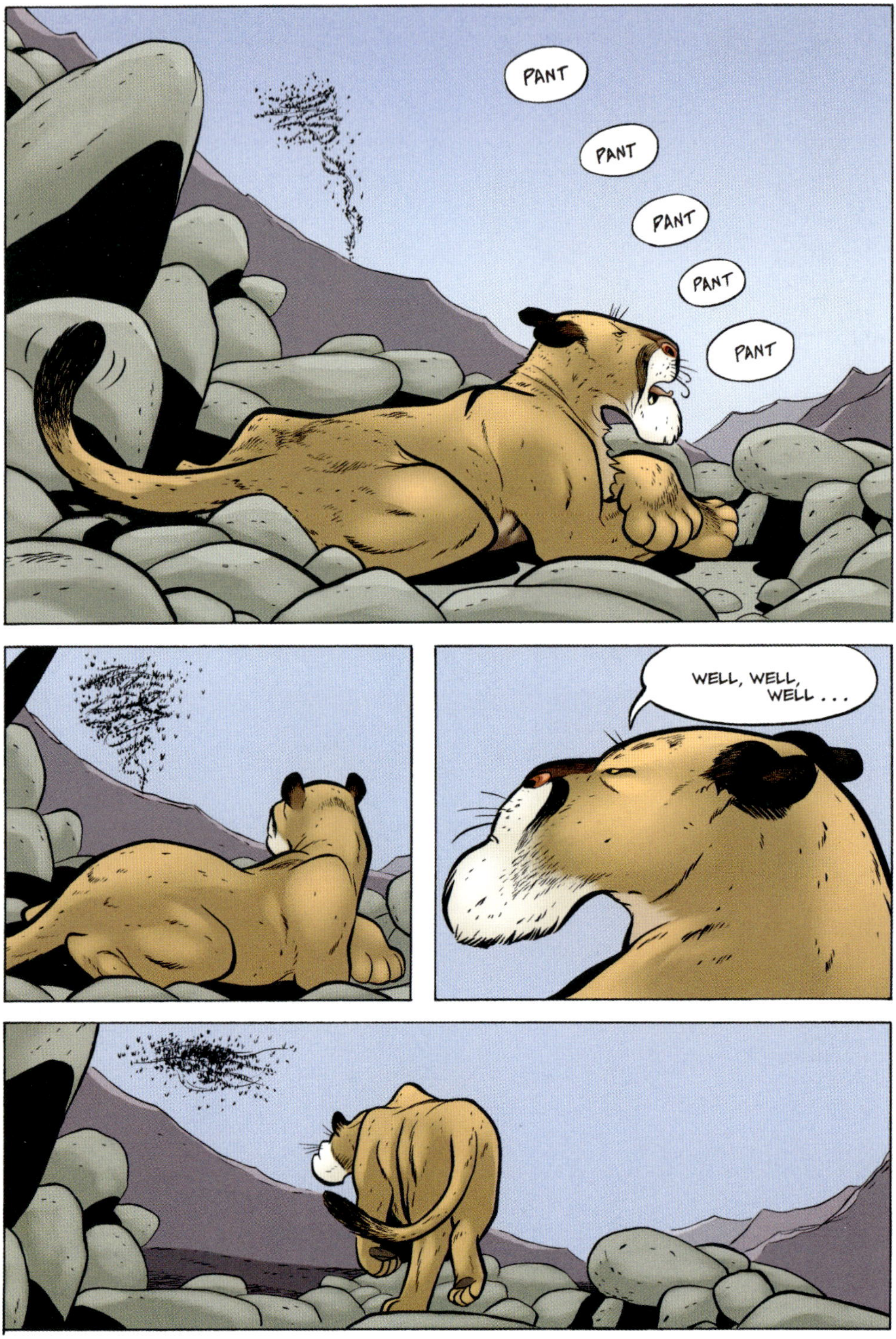

PANT
PANT
PANT
PANT
PANT

WHAT HAPPENED?!
SOMETHING FELL OUT OF BONE'S BACKPACK AND SCARED OFF THE LOCUSTS!

WHERE'S KINGDOK?
HE DISAPPEARED!
Poof! VANISHED INTO THIN AIR!
UUHN!

IS HE OKAY?
OW OOW.
MAN! I FELL ON THE EXACT SAME SPOT THAT JUST HEALED!

HEY! WHAT HAPPENED TO THE LOCUSTS?
SOMETHING IN YOUR BACKPACK SCARED THEM OFF! ARE YOU OKAY?
WHOA! CHECK IT OUT!

IT LOOKS LIKE A CROWN!
OOH!
A CROWN! I BET IT BELONGS TO THORN!
WHAT'RE YOU DOING WITH THAT IN YOUR BACKPACK, CUZ?

I HAD NO IDEA WHAT WAS IN THAT BUNDLE! GRAN'MA BEN GAVE IT TO ME AND ASKED ME TO KEEP IT SAFE!
WHAT ELSE IS IN THERE?
A GLOVE; SOME KINDA METAL SHIRT . . .
?

AND THIS! AN OLD MEDALLION!

HISS!
SSSS!
PUT IT AWAY!
WHAT'S THE MATTER?

THE MEDALLION! PUT IT AWAY!
IT IS A BAD THING!
HISS!
PUT IT AWAY, SMILEY.
OKAY, OKAY!

THAT IS WHAT SCARED THE LOCUSTS AWAY! IT IS A DRAGON-THING!
A DREAMING-THING!
A DREAMING-THING?
DREAMING IS PART OF THE LOCAL BELIEF SYSTEM.
GRAN'MA BEN WAS TELLING ME ABOUT IT.
MOBY DICK

YOU MEAN IT'S A RELIGION?
IT'S A RELIGION FOR GRAN'MA BEN AND THORN!
DREAMING IS A PEOPLE WORD! ANIMALS CALL IT HUM-HUM! IT'S THE HUM OF THE EARTH!

THE EARTH HUMS?
OF COURSE IT DOES! WHAT A RIDICULOUS QUESTION! DON'T YOU HEAR IT?

MMMMMM
NOPE. SORRY.
AW, C'MON! YOU GOTTA HEAR IT! HOW ELSE COULD YOU LEARN TO WALK, OR TALK OR FIND FOOD FOR YOURSELF?!

IF I DIDN'T LEARN IT IN TH' FOURTH GRADE, IT DIDN'T NEED LEARNIN'!
hmmf.
I HATE TO BREAK IT UP, GUYS, BUT WE CAN'T STAY HERE. WE'RE NOT SAFE UNTIL WE MAKE IT TO THE TREES!

WHAT ABOUT YOU, BONE? DO YOU HEAR IT?
WELL, ACTUALLY, WHERE WE COME FROM THERE IS NO HUM-HUM SO --
THAT'S NOT TRUE! IT'S EVERYWHERE! IT'S STRONGER IN SOME PLACES, BUT IT'S EVERYWHERE!
HE'S RIGHT!
DIDN'T YOU FEEL IT BACK AT THE OLD STONE TEMPLE?

OH, MAN, THE HUM-HUM'S ALWAYS CRAZY AT THE OLD TEMPLE, BUT TODAY IT WAS SCARY!
NO KIDDING! THAT WHOLE KINGDOK THING WAS INTENSE!
YEAH! DIDN'T HE LOOK REAL? I THOUGHT HE WAS REAL, UNTIL HE VANISHED!
?
YOU MEAN HE WASN'T REAL?

OH, MY GOSH! YOU THINK KINGDOK WAS PART OF A DREAM?!
OH, YEAH, FOR SURE! SOMETIMES WHEN YOU GO THROUGH THE TEMPLE YOU GET NIGHTMARES!
WHOA, WHOA.
ARE YOU SAYING KINGDOK WASN'T EVEN THERE?! WE JUST DREAMED IT?

YEAH! SEE? THAT'S HUM-HUM!
NOW JUST HOLD ON -- WHAT ABOUT ALL TH' ROCKS THAT WERE CRASHING DOWN AROUND US? THE LEDGE CRUMBLING OUT FROM UNDER OUR FEET?

THINGS GET CRAZY AROUND THAT OLD TEMPLE!
FOLKS SAY IT WAS BUILT ON A GHOST CIRCLE!
I BET IF WE WENT BACK, THE LEDGE WOULD BE IN ONE PIECE!
OH, COME ON! WE SAW IT -- WE FELT IT!

YOU CAN FEEL STUFF WHEN YOU DREAM!
!
MAN!
WHAT DID YOU SAY THIS TEMPLE WAS BUILT ON?

A GHOST CIRCLE! THAT'S WHERE THE LOCUSTS COME FROM.
VERY DANGEROUS! IF YOU STEP INTO ONE YOU'LL DISAPPEAR!
YOU GUYS ARE SERIOUS!
COOL!

SMILEY, THE GUY WHO'S AFTER PHONEY BONE - - - - HE'S CALLED THE LORD OF THE LOCUSTS!
RIGHT, RIGHT! HE PROBABLY CONTROLS THE LOCUSTS! HENCE TH' NAME!

I STILL DON'T UNDERSTAND HOW HE COULD INDUCE A MASS HALLUCINATION LIKE THAT.
MAYBE WE SHOULD GO BACK AND MAKE SURE PHONEY'S OKAY.

THIS GUY IS AFTER THORN, TOO! SHE DOESN'T HAVE ANY IDEA WHAT SHE'S UP AGAINST!
SHE'S COMPLETELY VULNERABLE!
I'LL SAY! THE LOCUSTS COULD MAKE HER BELIEVE ANYTHING! HECK! THEY COULD MAKE THE WHOLE VALLEY BELIEVE ANYTHING!

THAT'S IT! GRAB YOUR STUFF! WE HAVE TO GET BACK AND WARN OUR FRIENDS!
AYE, AYE, CAP'N!
YOU HEARD TH' MAN! LET'S ROLL!
MOBY DICK

YOU THERE! OPEN UP YOUR MOUTH!
WHY?

CHECKING FOR SMALL MAMMALS. ANYBODY IN THERE?
HELLO?
HELLO? HELLO?
OKAY, YER CLEAN!
C'MON, SMILEY! GET IT IN GEAR!

LET'S GET OFF THIS MOUNTAIN QUICK . . .
. . . BEFORE SOME NEW CRISIS REARS ITS UGLY HEAD!

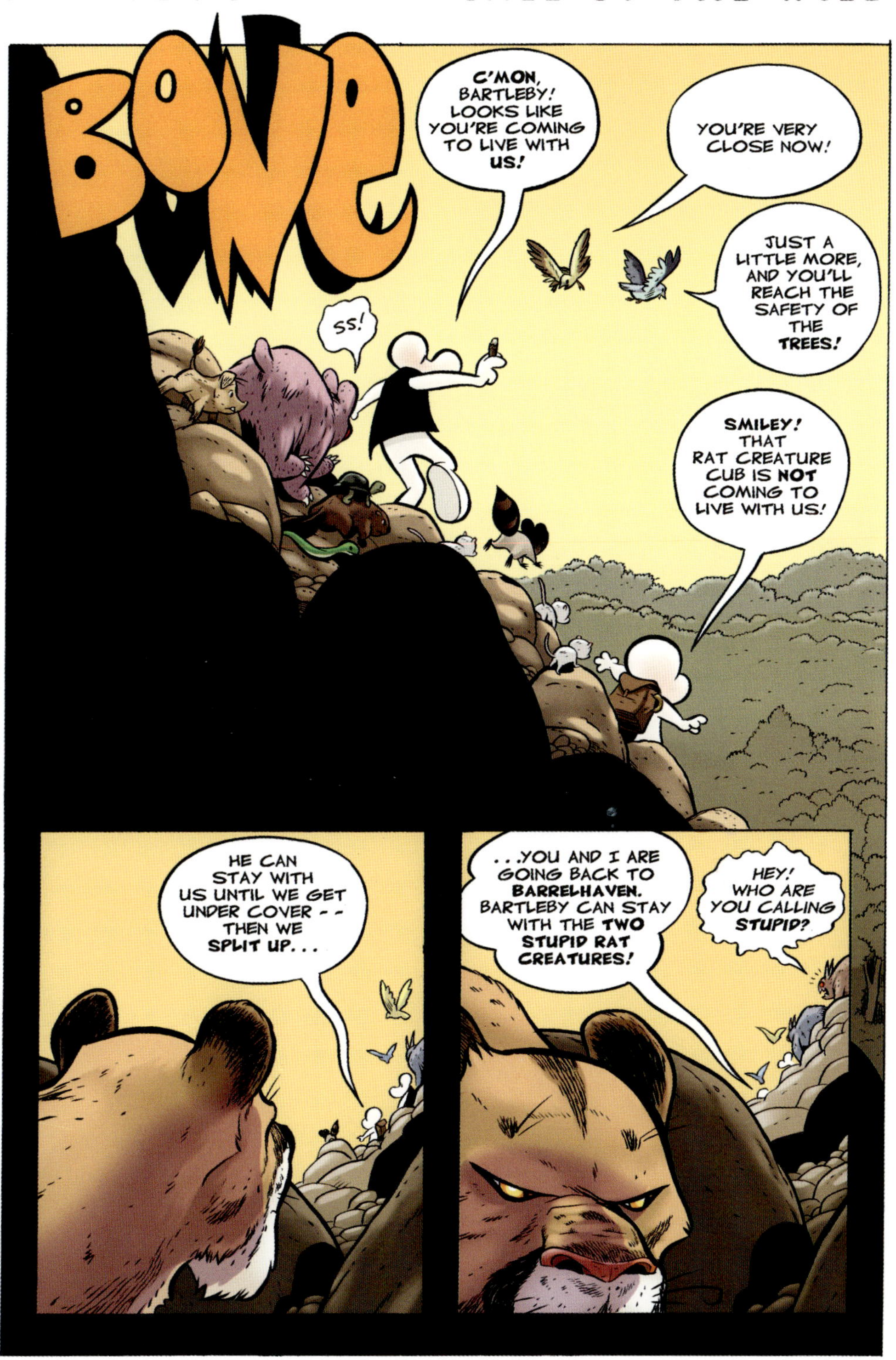
BONE
C'MON, BARTLEBY! LOOKS LIKE YOU'RE COMING TO LIVE WITH US!
YOU'RE VERY CLOSE NOW!
JUST A LITTLE MORE, AND YOU'LL REACH THE SAFETY OF THE TREES!
SS!
SMILEY! THAT RAT CREATURE CUB IS NOT COMING TO LIVE WITH US!
HE CAN STAY WITH US UNTIL WE GET UNDER COVER -- THEN WE SPLIT UP...
...YOU AND I ARE GOING BACK TO BARRELHAVEN. BARTLEBY CAN STAY WITH THE TWO STUPID RAT CREATURES!
HEY! WHO ARE YOU CALLING STUPID?

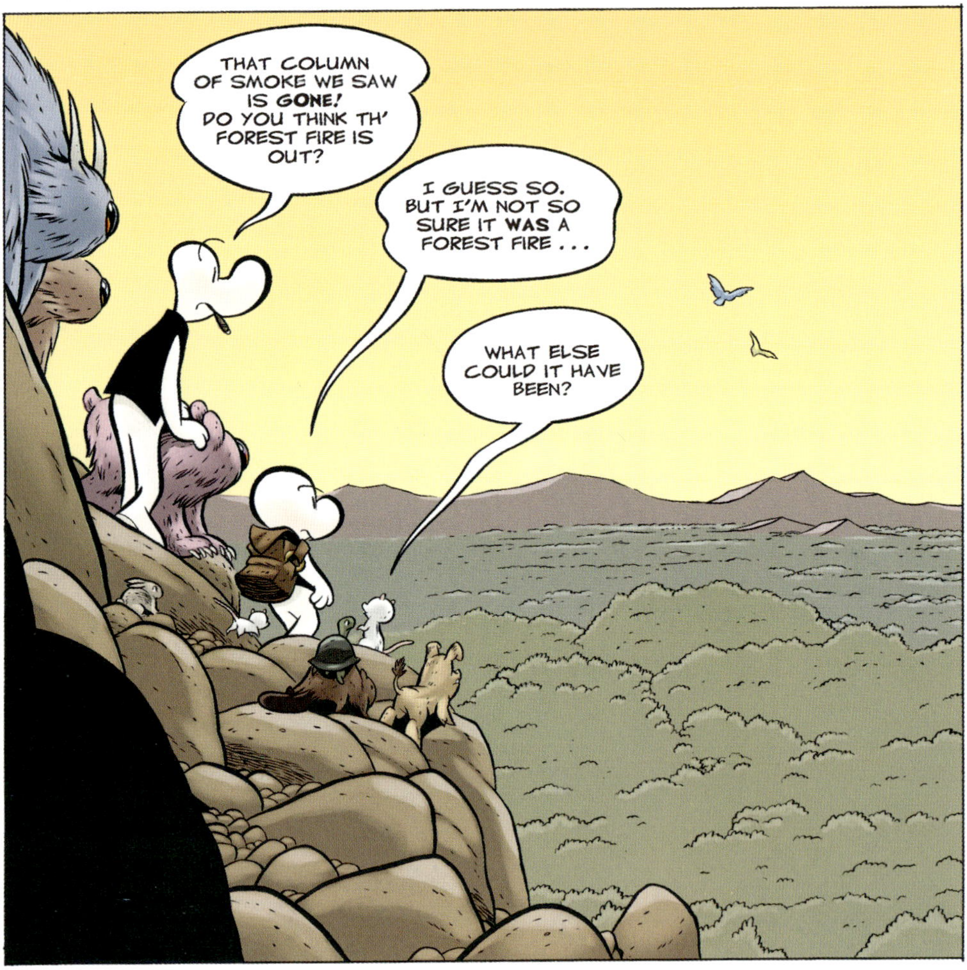

THAT COLUMN OF SMOKE WE SAW IS **GONE!** DO YOU THINK TH' FOREST FIRE IS OUT?

I GUESS SO. BUT I'M NOT SO SURE IT **WAS** A FOREST FIRE . . .

WHAT ELSE COULD IT HAVE BEEN?

I DON'T KNOW FOR SURE, BUT ALL OF ROCK JAW'S TALK ABOUT WAR IS MAKING ME KIND OF NERVOUS!

ROCK JAW! THAT OL' BLOWHARD! HE WAS SO FULL OF HIMSELF...

...BUT WE SHOWED THAT GIANT KITTY CAT, DIDN'T WE, KIDS?
YEAH! HA! HA!

I BET HE'S STILL AT THE TOP OF THE CLIFF GUARDIN' THE ENTRANCE TO THAT CAVE!
HEE! HEE! OL' ROCK JAW DOESN'T KNOW ABOUT OUR SECRET TUNNEL DOWN THROUGH THE OLD TEMPLE!

LET'S NOT CONGRATULATE OURSELVES JUST YET.
BESIDES, SMILEY, I'M MUCH MORE WORRIED ABOUT WHAT MAY HAVE HAPPENED IN THE VALLEY WHILE WE WERE AWAY.
OKAY, OKAY. STILL, I'D LIKE TO SEE THAT OL' RASCAL'S FACE WHEN HE REALIZES WE GAVE HIM TH' SLIP!

MR. BONE, IF YOU'RE WORRIED THAT SOMETHING MAY HAVE HAPPENED WHILE WE WERE GONE, WHY DON'T YOU ASK THE TWO RATS WE HAVE WITH US?
GOOD IDEA.

HEY, YOU TWO! WHAT DO YOU KNOW ABOUT THOSE COLUMNS OF SMOKE WE SAW DOWN IN THE VALLEY?
WE KNOW NOTHING! WE ARE ONLY LOWLY FOOT SOLDIERS ON BORDER PATROL!

BORDER PATROL?! THE FIRST TIME I MET YOU WAS ON THE OTHER SIDE OF THE VALLEY! YOU WERE DEEP IN DRAGON TERRITORY!
YES, YESSS, WE WERE BREAKING THE TREATY-- BUT KINGDOK COMMANDED US TO DO IT!

KINGDOK'S ADVISOR, THE HOODED ONE, TOLD HIM THAT A NEW LEADER WAS ENTERING THE VALLEY -- A LEADER WHO BORE A STAR ON HIS CHEST!
KINGDOK SENT US ACROSS THE VALLEY TO THE DRAGON'S STAIR TO CAPTURE THIS UPSTART THREAT!

THAT'S RIDICULOUS! OUR COUSIN PHONEY BONE IS NO LEADER! I CAN'T IMAGINE WHAT GAVE YOU GUYS THE IDEA HE WAS A THREAT!

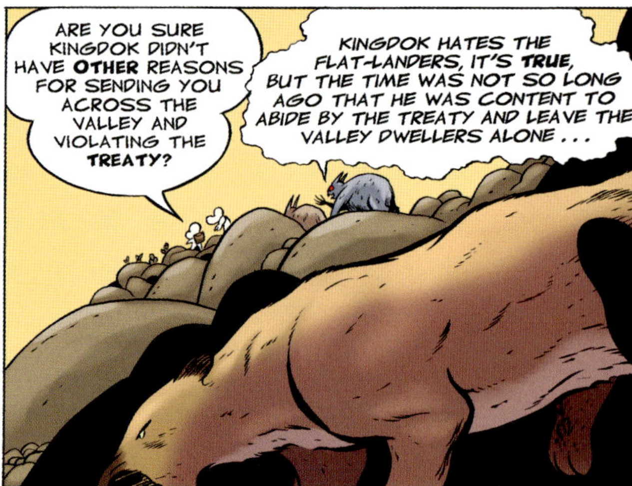
ARE YOU SURE KINGDOK DIDN'T HAVE OTHER REASONS FOR SENDING YOU ACROSS THE VALLEY AND VIOLATING THE TREATY?
KINGDOK HATES THE FLAT-LANDERS, IT'S TRUE, BUT THE TIME WAS NOT SO LONG AGO THAT HE WAS CONTENT TO ABIDE BY THE TREATY AND LEAVE THE VALLEY DWELLERS ALONE . . .

ALL THAT CHANGED WHEN THE HOODED ONE ARRIVED... HE CAME TO US FROM THE VALLEY... ONE OF THE WANDERING HOLY MEN KNOWN AS STICK-EATERS...

...AND WITH HIM CAME THE LOCUSTS AND THE DREAMS!

THE POWER OF THE LOCUSTS IS VERY STRONG!
YOU SAW IT TODAY AT THE OLD TEMPLE! THE DREAMS CAN MAKE YOU BELIEVE THE SKY ITSELF IS FALLING!

WITHOUT THE HOODED ONE TO CONTROL THE LOCUSTS, WE MIGHT ALL BE ROLLING SENSLESSLY ON THE GROUND, MAD AS LOONS!

CRIPES!
HMM.
MORE AND MORE KINGDOK LISTENS TO THIS STICK-EATER AND HIS LOCUSTS.
TO THE POINT THAT KINGDOK MUST OBEY THE HOODED ONE FOR FEAR THAT THE LOCUST WILL OVERWHELM HIM!
WE ALL MUST OBEY!

AND THIS IS THE KIND OF LIFE YOU WANT TO SEND LITTLE BARTLEBY BACK TO? SOME KIND OF INSECT CULT?
BARTLEBY IS A RAT CREATURE, SMILEY! IF THIS IS WHAT RAT CREATURES BELIEVE, THEN WHO ARE WE TO JUDGE?

IT WAS NOT ALWAYS SO. IN THE OLD DAYS THE HUM-HUM WAS GOOD. WE WERE HAPPY.
NOW WITH THE COMING OF THE LOCUSTS, IT IS DIFFICULT TO TELL WHAT IS GOOD. OR WHAT IS REAL.

THE HOODED ONE BLAMES OUR UNHAPPINESS ON THE VALLEY PEOPLE AND THE DRAGONS, AND ON THE TREATY WHICH FORCES US TO LIVE IN THE MOUNTAINS.

HE SAYS WE MUST RETURN TO THE OLD WAYS. . . TO THE TIME BEFORE THERE WERE VALLEY PEOPLE . . . WHEN THERE WAS ORDER IN THE WORLD.

YOU DON'T HAVE TO LISTEN TO THE HOODED ONE.
THAT'S RIGHT, HE'S NOT EVEN ONE OF YOU! IF YOU ASK ME, HIS MOTIVES ARE PRETTY SUSPECT!
IF WE DO NOT LISTEN TO HIM . . . HOW WILL WE BE HAPPY?

ONLY WHEN YOU TRULY UNDERSTAND THE HOODED ONE'S MOTIVES WILL YOU LEARN THE MEANING OF HAPPINESS . . .
WHO. . .?

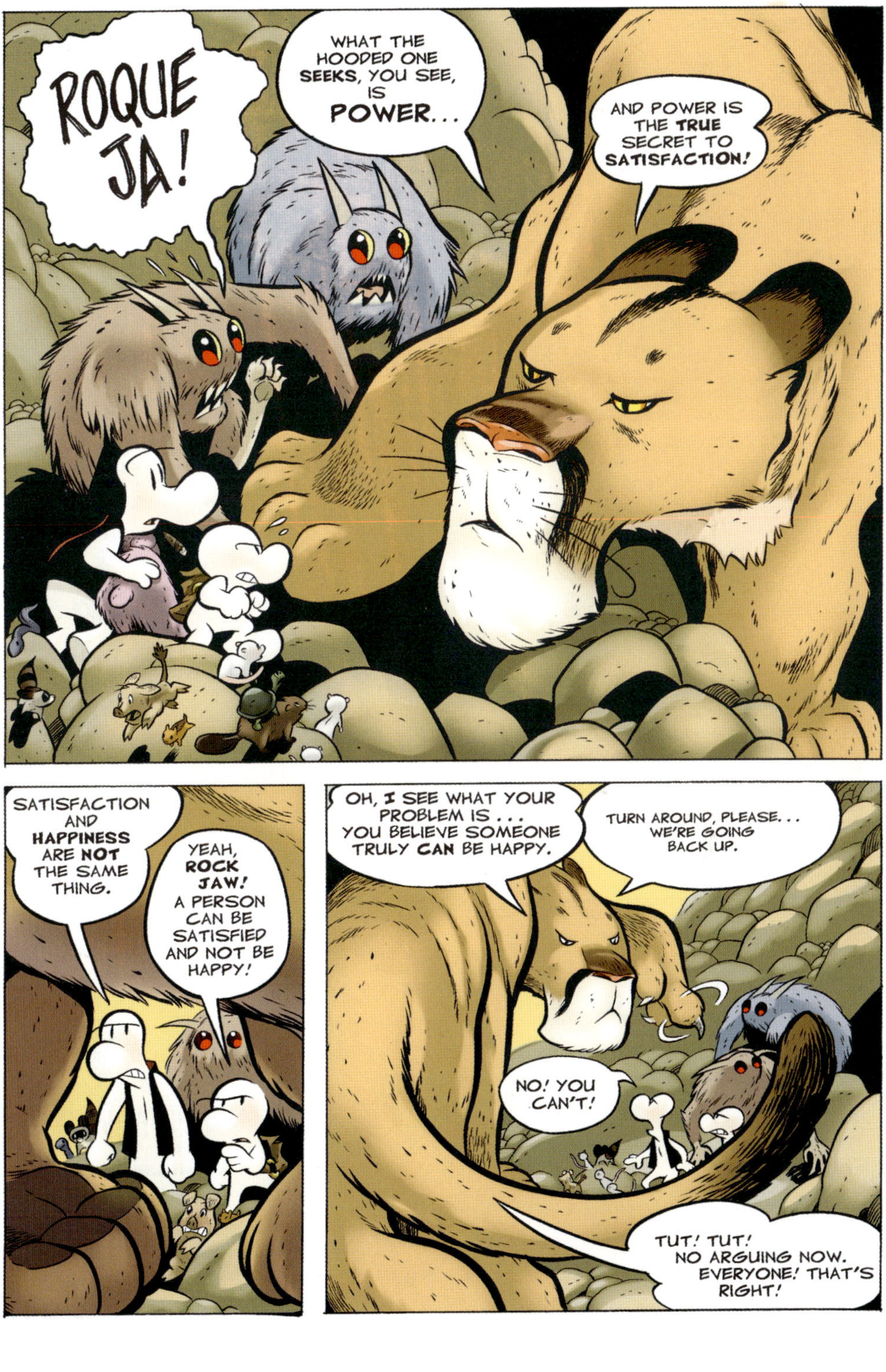

ROQUE JA!
WHAT THE HOODED ONE **SEEKS**, YOU SEE, IS **POWER**...
AND POWER IS THE **TRUE** SECRET TO **SATISFACTION**!

YOU SEE, HAPPINESS ITSELF IS JUST AN EMOTION THAT CAN BE INDUCED . . .
THE ONLY THING OF SUBSTANCE THAT MATTERS IS POWER!
WHAT ABOUT GOOD AND EVIL?

BAH! THERE IS NO GOOD AND EVIL. WHAT IS EVIL TO YOU DEPENDS ON WHAT SIDE YOU ARE ON. WHAT IS GOOD TO YOU IS EVIL TO THE RAT CREATURES, AND VICE VERSA.
THAT'S NOT TRUE!

ISN'T IT, MY LITTLE ORPHAN? DO YOU THINK THE SUN CARES IF YOUR MOMMA AND POPPA WERE EATEN BY RAT CREATURES? IT DOESN'T.

THE SUN WILL SET TONIGHT AND RISE AGAIN TOMORROW WHETHER YOU AND I ARE HERE OR NOT.

ANYTHING THESE MISERABLE WRETCHES DO IS UTTERLY INSIGNIFICANT.

THERE IS NO GOOD OR EVIL. . . ONLY NATURE. AND IN NATURE, THE ONLY THING THAT MATTERS IS POWER!

ONCE WE CROSS THIS PLATEAU AND START UP THAT PATH, WE WON'T GET ANOTHER CHANCE TO ESCAPE!
THIS IS IT, HUH?

WHAT'RE WE GONNA DO?!

YOU'RE WRONG, MR. ROCK JAW! THERE'S OTHER STUFF THAT MATTERS! LIKE FRIENDSHIP AND TRUST!
TAKE IT EASY, RODERICK! DON'T LET THAT BULLY GET TO YOU!

FRIENDSHIP AND TRUST ARE MERELY EARTHBOUND SENTIMENTS THAT ONLY LEAD TO TROUBLE. TRUST NO ONE, THAT'S MY MOTTO.

THE LIGHT WILL BE GONE SOON. IF WE CAN STALL HIM, WE MIGHT HAVE A CHANCE TO MAKE A BREAK IN THE DARK!
RIGHT!

UH, OH!
HEADS UP!
OUR ESCAPE PLAN JUST GOT COMPLICATED!

SSSS.
SSS
SSS
SSSS
SSS!
SSSS
SSSS!
!
!

IT'S **KINGDOK!**
OH, WE ARE IN BIG, **BIG** TROUBLE.

IS HE **REAL** THIS TIME?
OR IS IT A **DREAM?**
THIS SURE **FEELS** REAL!
UGH! IT **SMELLS** REAL!
SS!

HAIL, KINGDOK.
RRRRR. SSSSSS...
SSS!

TURN YOUR PRISONERS OVER TO US IMMEDIATELY!

TAKE THEM.
I WAS BRINGING THEM TO YOU ANYWAY!

WERE YOU.
PERHAPS YOU WERE EXPECTING A REWARD. . . ?
WELL. . .

HERE IS YOUR REWARD!

SNAP! SNAP!
HA! HA!
HA! HA! HA!

SNAP!
SNAP!
HA-HA
HA! HA!
HA! HA!
HA! HA!
HA-HA!
ROWWR!

HA! HA! MASTER OF THE EASTERN BORDER! LOOK AT HIM RUN!
HA! HA! HA!
HA! HA!
HA! HA!
HA! HA HA!

JEEZ! POOR ROCK JAW!
C'MON! LET'S GET OUTTA HERE!

HOLD IT!
OOK!
GRK!

LOOK, MASTER!
WE HAVE THEM!
YESS! YESSS! WE'RE NOT REALLY TRAITORS! WE WERE PLANNING TO HAND THEM OVER TO YOU THE WHOLE TIME!
GOOD, GOOD...
SSS
!
SSS
SSSS

QUICKLY! WE MUST BRING THEM BEFORE THE HOODED ONE!
THOSE DIRTY RATS!
GRR!
LET'S GO! THAT'S ALL I CAN TAKE!

CRUNCH!
AAIEE!
CHOMP!

AIII!
EEK!
BITE!
CRUNCH!
CHOMP!

RUN, YOU GUYS!
IT'S NOW OR NEVER!

STOP THEM!
Ooooh..
GO! GO!

HURRY! THEY'RE RIGHT BEHIND US!
SPLIT UP WHEN YOU HIT THE WOODS! EVERYBODY RUN AS FAST AS YOU CAN!
WE'RE ALMOST THERE!

NOT SO FAST.
AH!
LOOK OUT!

OVER HERE!
THIS WAY! THIS WAY!
LET'S GO!

HISSS!
EEK!
HELP! HELP!
UNDER HERE!

ZIP
POW!
BAM!

STAND ASIDE. I WILL CLEAR THEM OUT OF THERE.
EVERYONE! BACK UP! SQUEEZE IN AS FAR AS YOU CAN GO!!

RROWWWR
WUMP
ERR-
!
?!

ROW ROAAW!
IT'S ROCK JAW!
ATTA BOY, ROCK JAW! GIVE IT TO 'EM!

AAAARR
RUN FOR TH' TREES!
MOVE IT! THIS TIME WE'RE GOIN' HOME FOR REAL!

AAAAA..KK
AARR
GURGLE

EEK!
C'MON, RODERICK!
I'M COMIN'!

WE MADE IT! SPREAD OUT!
RUN AS FAST AS YOU CAN!

GOOD-BYE, 'POSSUMS! I'LL MISS YOU!
AREN'T YOU COMING WITH US?

NO, I LIVE IN THE MOUNTAINS. I'M STAYING HERE
THEN GOOD LUCK, RODERICK! THANKS FOR THE ADVENTURE!
YEAH, WE HAD A GREAT TIME!

HEY, YOU DORKS! YOU BETTER BREAK IT UP AN' GO HOME, OR YOU'RE GONNA BE SOMEBODY'S SUPPER!

GOODBYE FOR NOW! COME BACK TO TH' MOUNTAINS AN' VISIT ME!
WE WILL, RODERICK! GOODBYE!
GOODBYE!
GOODBYE!

I KNEW IT!
I KNEW OL' ROCK JAW WOULD TURN OUT TO BE ON OUR SIDE!

SMILEY, I DON'T THINK WHAT ROCK JAW DID HAD ANYTHING TO DO WITH US!
HEY!

WHAT?
OMIGOSH!

WHAT'S THE MATTER?
BARTLEBY!

WHERE'S BARTLEBY?

HE'S NOT RIGHT BEHIND US?
I DON'T SEE HIM!

UH, OH.
HE NEVER CAME DOWN!

C'MON! SOMETHING HAPPENED!
SMILEY! DON'T--!

BE CAREFUL! THERE'S GONNA BE RAT CREATURES ALL OVER THE PLACE!

THAT'S WEIRD... IT'S AWFUL QUIET.
LET'S PEEK OUT.

!

THERE'S NOBODY HERE!

THEY CAN'T JUST VANISH INTO THIN AIR!
YOU THINK IT WAS ANOTHER DREAM?!

NO - - WAIT! THERE THEY ARE! UP THERE!

THEY'RE LEAVING! AN' THEY'RE CARRYING KINGDOK AWAY!

LOOK AT THAT! THERE'S TWO GUYS RUNNIN' UP BEHIND THEM!

IT'S THE TWO STUPID RAT CREATURES!
THOSE BACKSTABBERS! THEY TRIED TO HAND US OVER AT TH' LAST MOMENT!

I WONDER WHAT THEY'RE UP TO?
MAYBE THEY'RE TIRED OF BEING DESERTERS.
SEEMS LIKE THEY'RE BEING ACCEPTED BACK INTO THE GROUP.
GOOD FOR THEM -- BUT WHERE'S BARTLEBY?
LOOK!

THERE HE IS!

WHAT'S HE DOIN'?!
HE'S TRYING TO REJOIN THE GROUP, TOO!

BUT I DON'T WANT HIM TO REJOIN TH' GROUP!
IT'S WHERE HE BELONGS, SMILEY! IT'S WHAT HE WANTS TO DO!

MMMMMM.
DON'T BE SAD!
IT'S WHAT WE CAME HERE TO DO! THIS IS A HAPPY ENDING!
NATURE HAS TAKEN ITS COURSE!

WILL HE BE OKAY?
YEAH. YEAH. HE'LL BE FINE.

LISTEN . . .
YOU CAN WATCH HIM FOR A WHILE IF YOU WANT, BUT NOT TOO LONG - - WE GOTTA GO, ALL RIGHT?
I GUESS.

GOOD-BYE, BARTLEBY.
I GOTTA GO NOW.

...TO BE CONTINUED.

About JEFF SMITH

JEFF SMITH was born and raised in the American Midwest and learned about cartooning from comic strips, comic books, and watching animated shorts on TV. After four years of drawing comic strips for The Ohio State University's student newspaper and co-founding Character Builders animation studio in 1986, Smith launched the comic book *BONE*® in 1991. Between *BONE*® and other comics projects, Smith spends much of his time on the international guest circuit promoting comics and the art of graphic novels.

More about *BONE*®

An instant classic when it first appeared in the U.S. as an underground comic book in 1991, Bone® has since garnered 38 international awards and sold a million copies in 15 languages. Now, Scholastic's GRAPHIX imprint is publishing full-color graphic novel editions of the nine-book *BONE*® series. Look for the continuing adventures of the Bone® cousins in *Rock Jaw: Master of the Eastern Border*.